*Coming up for Air*

# Coming up for Air

Poems by
Nancy Frederiksen

Paper Jack Creek Press
Coon Rapids, Minnesota • 2002

Coming Up for Air © 2002 by Nancy Frederiksen
Back cover photograph by Joni Pnewski
Cover photograph © 2002 by Nancy Frederiksen
Interior design by Donna Burch
Interior photographs courtesy Irene Sutliff

First Printing, 2002. All rights reserved.
No part of this book may be reproduced without
written permission of the author and publisher.
Printed and bound in the United States of America.

The author wishes to express gratitude to The Loft, Minneapolis, Minnesota whose writing workshops, classes and events are a constant reinforcement to a writer's life. She would also like to thank the Harmony Women's Fund for a residency at Norcroft Retreat on Lake Superior during which time some of these poems took shape. Special thanks to the author's writing partners Tom Heie, Karen Karsten, and Zilla Sherritt Way who have always been encouraging and supportive, and to designer Donna Burch whose expertise helped make this vision a reality.

Library of Congress Control Number: 2002094047
Frederiksen, Nancy
Coming Up For Air : poems / by Nancy Frederiksen.
ISBN 0-9656210-1-4

For personal orders or other information, please write to:
Paper Jack Creek Press
P. O. Box 48944
Coon Rapids, MN 55448-0944

# *Acknowledgements*

Grateful acknowledgement is made to the following publications in which some of these poems first appeared: *ArtWord Quarterly* ("Onions"); *Calyx, A Journal of Art and Literature by Women, Vol. 19, no. 3, Winter 2000/2001* ("Bobbie, 1945"); *Great River Review* ("Silence"); *Murmurs of the Past, a Guild Press anthology* ("His Chair"); *Rag Mag* ("Braided Rugs," "Skinning Muskrat," "Freedom," "A Taste For Chocolate" and "Your Ways, Father"); *Roaring Muse, UMD Literary Guild* ("The Other World"); *Sidewalks* ("Bookshelf," "Invisible Fish" and "Translation"); *The North Stone Review* ("Gladiolus" and "Emergence").

*to my family, for the stories*

*and in memory of*

*mother, Irene H. Sutliff, 1912–2002*
*father, Chester G. Sutliff, 1902–1977*

# Contents

## *Homeward Bound*
Homeward Bound .................................................. 3
White Space ............................................................ 4
His Chair ................................................................. 5
Ties that Bind ......................................................... 6
Gladiolus ................................................................. 7
Escape ..................................................................... 9

## *Invisible Threads*
Braided Rugs ........................................................ 13
Long Distance ...................................................... 14
Lace Drawbacks ................................................... 15
Still Life ................................................................ 17
Breathless ............................................................. 18
Early Rain, Leftover Ice ...................................... 20
Broken Bones ....................................................... 21
Sacrifice ................................................................ 22
Onions ................................................................... 23
Legacy ................................................................... 25

## *Filling in the Garden*
Odd Couple .......................................................... 29
Your Ways, Father ............................................... 30
Driving Lessons ................................................... 31
Lucky Daddy ........................................................ 32
Filling in the Garden ........................................... 33
If I Had a Hammer .............................................. 34
Translation ........................................................... 35

## *Capturing the Animal*
Freedom ................................................................ 39
Trapping ............................................................... 41
Skinning Muskrat ................................................ 42
Invisible Fish ....................................................... 43
Casting .................................................................. 44

Hunting Vest ............................................................. 45
Duck Hunting ........................................................... 46
Things We Carry ....................................................... 48
Falcon ....................................................................... 49

## *Traffic Signs*
Bobbie, 1945 ............................................................. 53
Coming Up For Air ................................................. 54
Sweet Pea Season ..................................................... 55
Edges ......................................................................... 57
Ride Like the Wind ................................................. 59

## *Full of Nerve*
Flying Blue Angel .................................................... 63
The Other World ..................................................... 64
Leather Jacket .......................................................... 65
Halloween ................................................................. 66
Speech ....................................................................... 67
Thrill Seeker ............................................................. 69
Bookshelf .................................................................. 70

## *In Search Of*
A Taste for Chocolate .............................................. 73
The Hunt for Asparagus ......................................... 74
Downstream ............................................................. 76

## *Breathing Lessons*
Emergence ................................................................ 79
Vacation .................................................................... 80
Breathing Lessons .................................................... 81
Silence ....................................................................... 82

"I should not talk about myself if there were anybody else whom I knew so well. Unfortunately, I am confined to this theme by the narrowness of my experience. Moreover, I, on my side, require of every writer, first or last, a simple and sincere account of his own life, and not merely what he has heard of other men's lives; some such account as he would send to his kindred from a distant land; for if he has lived sincerely, it must have been in a distant land to me."

Henry David Thoreau

# Homeward Bound

## *Homeward Bound*

You're surrounded
by storms and warnings,
trees down,
branches strewn.

Cars slow,
creep through water
too deep to rush through.
Jagged lightning and
cracking thunder flash
and pierce the weakening
ozone layer. Enter a new world,
not comfortable
but in the midst of a storm,
driving home in the rain.

You keep driving in spite
of the storm, in spite of
deep pockets of water,
the level of fear rising and
cresting as you inch your way.
You watch other travelers:
dare to go as they go.

You think you should pull over,
wait for the rain to subside,
but the water is deep and getting
deeper. It won't get any better
until you've gone through it.

An intense desire to get home
has its hands at the wheel
holds your breath, takes you
through the deepening drive.

# *White Space*

In a trance of immediate need
I drive through a blizzard.

On I-94, a windswept
exit, lack of pavement,
drifted and turning road.
If it gets any worse, the exit
will close.

It does get worse.

More white space:
nine miles of country roads
leading to the driveway
in front of our house where
the ambulance pulls out
with Father in it.

And more white space:
sheets tucked white over white
open gowns, white
uniforms, dripping
tubes, one last breath
then one last call
Mother's voice
the final news.

Eyes beyond loss
see outside. Around a
lamppost, snowflakes
swirl in a vacuum,
lightly dance
in the dark.

## His Chair

The living room shrank
after Dad had the ceiling
lowered and the chair he sat in
never moved, except for
cleaning time.

His corner of the world,
the morning paper, a ritual,
the worn green footstool,
the gilted ashtray stand.

Even when she had to make room
for the Christmas tree,
Dad's chair faced the TV.
Sports car racing with Bobbie
Unser, Johnnie Rutherford,
the studied golf swings of
Arnold Palmer—he ate his
home-cooked meals on TV trays
cursed the Vikings
cheered the Packers.
Mom stopped getting the paper
after Dad died.

She even moved the chair.

# *Ties That Bind*

Given three months to live
Dad claimed his chair as home.
Christmas loomed, now an
empty tradition—except for
the one gift he loved, a bathrobe
from Mom—soft, velour,
something he could sink into.

Years later Mom
gave the robe to my brother.
He waited a long time to put it on.
He got the gold watch too, that
commemorative pat-on-the-back
for 25-years service.

Today when Mom gave me
Dad's tie clip, she surrendered
a simple gold design,
two straight lines, a delicate chain.

I keep it clipped to my checkbook.
A reminder of Dad's value system.
A checkpoint for mine.

## *Gladiolus*

When Father was alive he
brought in flailing arms of
stems from the garden: 48 years
of consecutive & intermittent
    blossomings & seasons.

Now, for Mother's 80th birthday,
we give her what we can
    of her past
in clear water & generous vases.

We allow the stems to fall
    as they may, much
as we came into this world:
    haphazard, taken in.

When the party was
over, I ended up with these,
    the lightest colors,
for all the others were
    spoken for—
the deep purple, bright yellows,
    rich reds, bright whites.

On my table, pale lilac frilled
edges turn to ivory centers,
a delicate turning in,
then the darkness of retreat.

## *Escape*

A deer shot across the road
in front of the car
quick as a gasp
and before the next breath
a smaller version
scurried behind
*like Mother followed*
*the footsteps of*
*Father who always*
*knew what to do*
*heeded his words*
*followed him into*
*his forest, that*
*pocket of desire,*
*that familiar home.*

Two deer had come
out of nowhere
surprising me
like cancer
and before I knew it
the forest had swallowed
them whole—
the deer, the father

and behind me I saw
the white tail of flight
flicking & flipping
defiant & definite.

# Invisible Threads

## *Braided Rugs*

She saved wool rags.
Kept them in brown paper bags
in the upstairs attic. When
the walls of the bags tore
and remnants spilled onto
slats of the grey painted floor
she brought them

downstairs
cut them into inch-and-a-half
wide strips, enlisted our help
(every girl ought to know
how to sew)
braided the strips
then sewed the braids
by hand.

Years later
one braided rug remains.
Woven and twisted
wool suit pants
flannel pajamas
red hunting shirts
sewn together in
soft and scratchy mixtures

remnants of generations
millions of
invisible threads.

## *Long Distance*

Mother calls me late at night and
we come at each other like strangers
searching for common ground,
fertile land.

She begins with a story but
I am tired and cannot listen.
My ears are full. The day was long.

The lines crackle and hiss.
Hanging up, before the final click,
I hear in her voice, her trailing goodbye,
the real distance between us
hovering like a thief.

Time, with its ever turning motion,
taking her away.

# *Lace Drawbacks*

Mom stands under the archway,
fixed in my mind like concrete.
I stand on a wooden ladder
threading lace curtains through
a rusted rod.

The curtains had hung to dry
earlier on lines south of the house.
Dirt from those lines rubbed off.
Mom wasn't sure where the spots were.

I watched for them as we crisscrossed
the lace drawbacks. "Epsom salt," she
says, she uses a little of that to
get them stiff. And then we come
to the spot of dirt which I show her
then point out how perfect it is
that it will be hidden in the folds
where the tieback pulls the lace
to the edge of the window.

But all my words won't hide the dirt.
She knows where it is.
Always will.

## *Still Life*

Mother holds a photo—
her Mother in a
Victorian dress,
neckline to the chin,
buttons all the way up,
then lets the secret out:

"There was a baby
Grandma went off to have
before Grandpa came around
and he married her *anyway*,
raising one that was not his own."

This is Mother's picture:
*the knight in shining armor
saves damsel in distress.*

She holds it up,
a shining example.

Believes the legend, still.

## *Breathless*

She hid postage stamps in the china cabinet
forgot where she put them
and could never have a cup of coffee
without a roll.
I want to see her now more often than I did
when I was young and vowed never to be
forgetful or fat.

I want to laugh and plan garage sales
forget about Bobbie's death, buy doughnuts.
I want to shake the past from our skin
like she shook the rugs Saturday morning
snap out all the dust.

She calls me Patty, Jeanne, Virgie
sometimes Nancy
scrambles brothers names the same.

I remember walking to the corner store,
me so small
and she walked so fast.
I'd take three steps to her one
and hurry she'd say. I'd hurry.

Now I go to the corner store alone
in a different town, different state
hurry through the aisles
pick up milk, corn, potatoes.

And I walk in her footsteps
but can't catch up.
There's more I haven't got
and so much time in her voice.

## *Early Rain, Leftover Ice*

Mother slips on ice going out to
get the mail, gives birth to me
a month before my time.
The stage is set for resistance
when she forces an issue
and that becomes our pattern.

Today I ask how to make lefse,
hear a slip of joy in her
eagerness, see it again in the
stance she takes at the griddle
becoming Mother, holder of the stick
turner of flattened pieces
leaving them on the griddle
until brown spots appear like
on an aging hand.

Time has need of its pleasure,
its turn at completion.

She flicks a cloth over the pieces
dusts flour from the surface
shows me how it's done then tastes it
too soon off the griddle.
Offers a piece to me.

I have a choice this time
to wait until it's ready.
This time she gives me
that freedom.
And I take it.

## *Broken Bones*

She has broken her arm, tripped over a throw rug
by the back porch door near the painted cupboard
where she keeps the turkey roaster.
She wants to go to the nursing home.
We do as she says. Check her in.

Quick to give orders, she now takes them.
We see dependence grow like a shadow.
When her 97-year-old roommate talks
about having a baby, as if she could,
Mom sees this as a sign—time to leave.

She checks herself out and at home,
practices lifting her arms,
inch by inch, day by day.

Home-care workers come to the house.
She tells them to dust
where to find the vacuum.
Just exactly what to do

with those throw rugs.

# *Sacrifice*

Fish. Fish. Sunfish.
She'll fix them up for me.
I'm coming to see her.
    She has plans.

Coffee. Morning.
    Stopped plans.
I go to see her.
She has fish for me.
She'll fry them up.

I am going to see her
& my plans are thwarted.
    Fish. Fish.
The table is set.
A plate for her.
A plate for me.

At the table she
pulls out bones,
relishes large portions
of flakey white meat
then tells me she
had to give that up
to us kids when we
were young—"and I got
this" she says and
holds up a tail piece,
then drops it to her plate.

Fish. Sunfish.
She pushes the plate to me.
I eat more than I want.

The bones begin to gather.

# *Onions*

Mom sent along an onion.
Stuck it on top of
macaroni in a small
Corningware dish.
Two hamburgers, too.
Wrapped in buns and
microwaveable plastic.

I'd gotten used to salads.
Crabmeat and croutons.
The lightness of separating
my life from my past
bacon grease from bacon.

I will eat these gifts slowly.

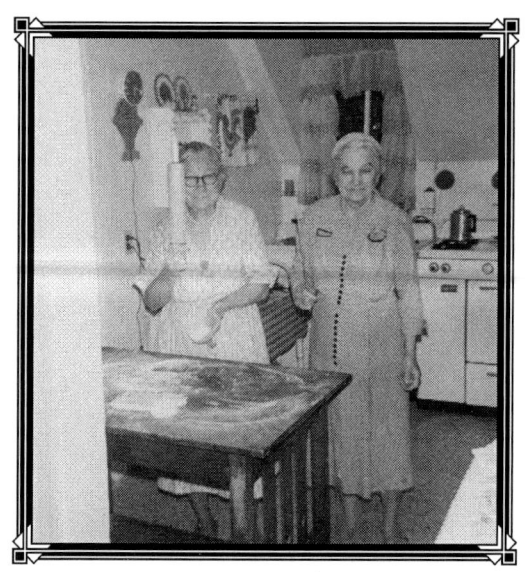

The Lefse Sisters

# *Legacy*

They want rosettes, a delicate pastry of the patient
Norwegian and give the irons to me.
They search for someone to carry on
the ways of the Old Country.

I am of my Mother who is of her Mother
who came from the Old Country
across the sea with a husband, a trunk and an
apron. The apron strings are too tight for me.
I untie the knot. Loosen hold of the past
(but the irons are still in the closet).

I try to make rosettes but have lost the recipe and call
Mother. "Are you writing this down?" she asks.
"Yes, Mom, I am."

I try to get them to drop off the iron but they stick.
She tells me how hot the oil should be,
how to hold the iron down 'til they're
bubbling to the top like excited children.

One rises like a child off to college.
I pull it from the fire.

Heat does not alter
intricate Norwegian patterns.

# Filling in the Garden

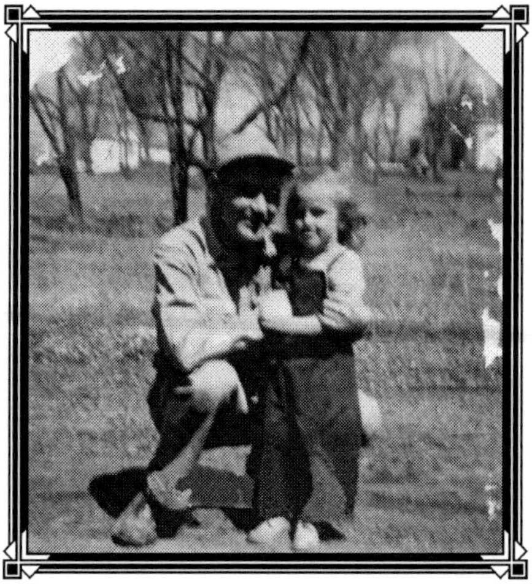

# *Odd Couple*

At the kitchen table, Father debated
whether or not to teach me cribbage.
The board with its drilled and empty
holes lay between us, a challenge.
Mother said, "Go ahead, why not?"

I caught on to the counting, the score, the game,
then beat him two out of three.
He packed up the cards, clacked them
on the table and said "that's it . . ."
The games were over.

The whiskered face of
Walter Matthau
unveiled itself beneath
the mask of Father.

The games were just beginning.

## *Your Ways, Father*

Your sullen looks, the crabapple
dismissal when I'd win
too many games

the grumbling from your chair
and the wait for a quarter
I knew you would give

but the suspense that held
us captive until you would give it up
like a gold medallion we were to
treasure.

It was spent, quickly spent
on movies and candy. Gone.

But not forgotten
is the suspense.

We learned to think of it as love.

# *Driving Lessons*

Father takes me down country roads
to idle at the edge of grass and snow.
He tells me of gears, timing, clutch
and release, then lets me take the wheel.

His voice takes on an edge when I round
the corner, sharp as the ice he thinks is there.
Words land against the windshield, bounce
back broken. I stop the car, he drives home.

Mother holds the door open.
Her hand grazes my tear-stained cheek.
I rush past. Words fall out of his
mouth, land at my back: "Stick to
what you're good at."

I sew a blouse that night, pay
close attention to how well I do,
round each corner, take control,
drown out his television,
his programming.

Make a lot of noise.

## *Lucky Daddy*

he took us to the side
of the road
to find blackberries

blueberries he had us on
our knees for

but mostly I remember
four-leaf clovers

how easily he found them
how they reached up to him
as if to say

    pick me
    pick me
    pick me

## *Filling in the Garden*

turn back the soil
like Father did
break up the clumps
again and again
come at it with
sharp edges of
hoe
noun
verb

bulb by bulb
word
by
word
pushing through

## *If I Had A Hammer*

This hammer
becomes a screwdriver
then a phillips
when you twist the
handle *(like the
small silver one
Dad kept in the
toolbox on the
wooden shelf
in the basement)*.

I put my plastic card
on the counter.
I *must* purchase this.
I must *have* this piece
of my past.

Two sisters talk.
How would Dad ever
get credit?—he paid cash
all his life! Then laughter.

I transcend.
Get all the credit I can.
Take years to hammer down the debt.

# *Translation*

Take it off my shoulder
the red, heavy wooden ladder
that slid alongside the roof
when wind pushed it down.

Let it go somewhere else this time:
not to Father's arm up to stop its fall
not to my head, where it bounced
not to the shoulder of my brother

no hospital ride in the back seat of
the car, no saltines & 7-Up
as I recuperate on the bed

no sympathy that for years
translates
*Father saves Daughter.*

His arm was up to save himself.

I still find it hard to believe.

# Capturing the Animal

# *Freedom*

Father beckons me to
follow him down the basement
stairs though I am headed
somewhere else. I stand
in front of a two-plank
workbench, holding a muskrat
for him to skin. There is
no way I can get out of this.

The air is still & damp,
his concentration intense.
He positions the blade carefully
at the intersection of meat
and skin, slides it along
precise: a clean cut.

I grip the leather claws
as he pulls the hide
from the carcass that is
my end to hold.

It is my responsibility to do this.
I can't let him down.
I am the daughter who will hang on
to the very end

when he tugs at the skin to get
it taut by the hind feet
then slices the last connection
to free the animal
from its skin.

"He goes trapping every year that Wisconsin has an open season and while he takes advantage of all of the nearby woods and streams that are his within a five-mile radius, he also, at the same time, makes use of all the modern conveniences of this modern age."

*(From the January-February 1953 issue of The Doughboy Sun)*

# *Trapping*

Down the woods of snow-crusted
wind-blown drifts,
Father at 74 explored
riverbanks and frozen terrain
for rusted clamping traps
laid out the day before.

If there was a muskrat
without breath in its
furred and freezing body,
the trophy was his.
Outcunning the cunning
was his game.

If there was life left,
he was destined to save it.

After a second heart attack
Mother wouldn't let him to go alone.
Went so far as to go with him—
stayed in the car
while he checked the traps.

If there was life left,
she was destined to save it.

## *Skinning Muskrat*

a clean sharp cut of knife
slit skin away from meat

mink and muskrat fur
hang upside down inside out
on thin slats of shaped boards
to stretch and dry

I think of shiny fur
and the slick animal wet from
cold streams

I think of the time he
caught a muskrat by the paw
and took him home to heal

I think of speed and cunning
hold cold leathery feet

watch the coat being
taken off
by an expert skinner

## *Invisible Fish*

A mist rolls over the lake this morning
as haunting as memories that linger.
It has lifted some since I first woke.

The last of it—a brief
reminder dissipating.

Ah, that it would be that
easy to evaporate,
lift like the joy of the invisible fish

the splash I heard
the ripple I saw seconds later.

Think how he dives after such a leap
through lily pad roots tangled

to the murkiness
he swims through

dark
he swims through

always
he swims through.

## *Casting*

A sideways flick of the wrist
whipped flyrod back, sent
transparent line and tied fly
downstream.

He lifted the lid once
slid three trout
from his woven basket
to the grass at my feet
so proud of his catch.

Always in the freezer:
speckled trout
in milk cartons
captured in time.

Today at the restaurant:
a speckled trout on the menu.

A thin line thrown out—
it catches me.

## *Hunting Vest*

After Dad died, my brother took his
hunting vest home, filled the
slots with bullets, taught his dog
to retrieve.

I think about hunters
driving bullets into birds
about hollow sounds, narrow tunnels
and forced entrances. I think
about the path a bullet takes
the way it explodes
near the heart.

I remember finding chips of
buckshot, the sound of them
landing on my plate
a tinking plop
not unlike
the sound of a duck's bill
after the hunt
carcass tossed on a bench
top and bottom bills
clacking together.

An odd echo.
A dry wild taste.

# *Duck Hunting*
### *(after reading Nikki Giovanni)*

a canvas vest
hanging on a hook

Father's vest
Father's canvas vest
hanging on a hook

limp now
limp now
limp now that he's
gone

gone
like the ducks
he shot

duck hunter
driving pellets
into birds

into live birds
into birds that we eat

hunger driving us
like a bullet

that lands
in a bird
in a bird that we eat
in the chest of a bird that we eat

exploding
in the chest
in the chest that they opened
the doctors
the chest that they opened
to find the buckshot

no, the chest that they
opened to find the cancer

the same chest
I sat against
leaned on
trusted

the same chest
that took a breath
before taking a shot

and his aim was sure
his vision complete
the bird would fall
the bird would fall

## *Things We Carry*

The path is wider than I expect.
No brush along the way.

We cross a stream where
four ducklings
without their mother
come from one protected cove
and go into another.

We see the funnel web of a spider
which starts out large and
narrows down to an opening
where the spider waits.

Under a gathering of pines
we look for owl pellets, a
pile of what the owl gives up
after a night of feeding:
small skulls, teeth and bones.

At the creekbed, we find the
lava rock we came for and
gather the best in a pile.
The greed in our bones wants
more than we can carry.

The same path that took us in
will take us out. Where the
slope was once downhill,
it is now, each step,
taking my breath away.

## *Falcon*

We watch the sky turn black,
swirling dark over luminous light.
Opposites in the spectrum
coming face to face,

an encounter creating an
easily understood line
of demarcation, a clear
difference. Something
you can defend.

A falcon swoops from the right
down and up to the left
excited
and all present

lose their breath
let it out in waves
as the raptor
falls below their sight
and rises above their vision

slicing in its
wildness of flight,
breaking in its defiance
of blackening skies.

# Traffic Signs

## *Bobbie, 1945*

Thick and unruly bushes prevent a driver
from seeing my brother who dashes in
front of the truck for a rubber band
snapping out of his hand, flinging
onto the tar, his small and anxious
fingers wanting to snatch it back.

Inside the house, my sister drops a
dinner plate. A pattern is broken.

No one hears the scream that
tangles in her breast, settles like fog
through which she runs to gather
her brother then later gives the news
to Father who works for the company
that owns the truck that couldn't stop.

I think of the silence they cultivated
the words they could not say.

I think of the brother I never had
Mother at her factory job
and the sister who watched out
the window as if it were a movie.

I think of silence and the heavy
laden sigh when we bring the topic
to the table, how we sit listening
taking it all in. Not wanting to take it in
but wanting the truth,
so hungry for it, we stop eating.

# *Coming Up For Air*

The dirt was loose but they had
climbed this hill before:
neighbor boys flipping coins,
kings of the backyard hill.
It wasn't until the ledge caved in,
they felt the earth give way.

"Jackie's buried in the dirt behind the
house by the hill!" My brother, John,
came running for help, his voice piercing
Dad's sleep who ran with a shovel
to dig Jackie out, whose feet were
planted like a flag, upside down waving,
to show Dad where they were—at attention.

How hard it had been to be careful and fast.
To sculpt the hidden shape.

There must have been a pocket, an open space
a crack in the earth that saved his lungs,
spread them apart like wings
when the avalanche fell in around his face,
a mask he would wear several minutes.

When Jackie's mother pulled him from
the hole, she laid him on the grassy bank,
reached in his mouth, dug out the dirt.
Bit by bit she opened channels
as a doctor does a newborn.
Not knowing if it was too late.
Not giving it a thought.

## *Sweet Pea Season*

Every summer sweet pea trucks
passed our house on Highway 65
headed for Friday Canning
where extra help was hired
in the summer then let go
when canning season was done.

We'd run up behind the truck
grab handfuls of fresh green
vines hanging out the back
and pull the trailing ends
to get a good bunch

while the drivers slowed
for us. We didn't know
they had to slow down
in front of the house—
the speed limit changed.

We just thought how
wonderful it was, that
people would be so willing
to give us what we wanted.

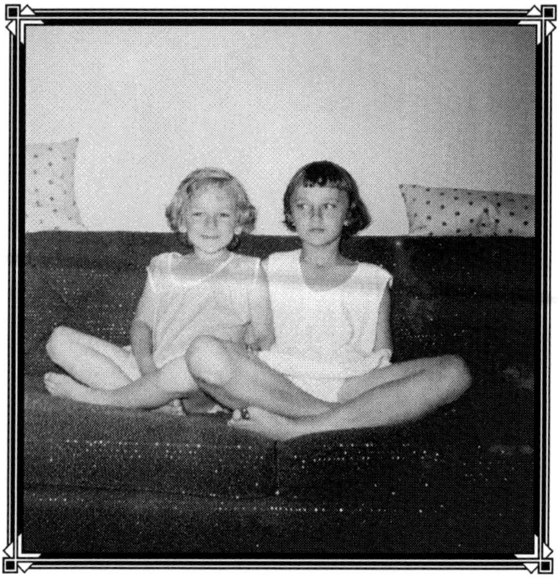

# *Edges*

My sister and I heard at night
th—thump, th—thump
first front wheels, then back
cars passing over a seam in the road.

We saw at night
a blinking light
on and off, on and off
a speed limit warning
flashing flashing

at the edge of town.
Our bedroom window faced
the road to the Cities—

the future, the blinking
blinking
future.

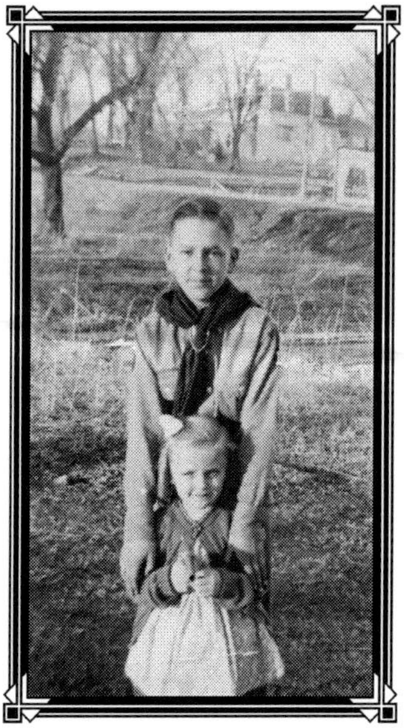

## *Ride Like the Wind*

I am learning to handle a dirt bike
on gravel; the bounce and grit of it,
dust and wind of it.
Older brother is watching.

I am learning balance and what
happens when people are watching.
Performance and the wind of choice,
a desperate combination.

There is a road but I don't take it.

When I disappear into the veil
of a willow, he holds his breath.
When I burst through the leaves
like Evil Knievel, he

laughs at how I crash in a heap
at his feet, then rise
to brush the dirt from
my clothes.

In the house, Mother swears.

# Full of Nerve

## *Flying Blue Angel*

You were leader of the pack
and it had been brave of me
to trust in you,
meet you at the rink
lace our skates
in the warming house
tune our rhythm to the
*Flying Blue Angels* crackling
from a make-shift loudspeaker
hooked to the top of an old car.

Freshman year, Mother said
"tell that boy good-bye"
and I handed out her verdict.
You took it as if it belonged
to you, fit like a second skin.

Years later, the woman you
married left
with bruises traced back to you,
further back then to your father.
Did the hand that held mine, do that?

My heart disbelieves
remembers
only the music
*daredevils of the sky*
arms linked in trust

hearts wide open.

# *The Other World*
*(in memory of Terri Lynn Davis)*

The teen that drove the car
that hit them
pulled out in front
of Terri and her friend in '92.

Mother, the bearer of bad news
calls to tell me this.

After a shower meant to cleanse
I heard a happy song on the radio
and I hoped then Terri heard it too.

Then that song, that electric
circuited radio
broke up into pieces
of static
like glass shattering.

I heard the crash
in that space of time
and it wasn't static
it was moving
swift as a motorcycle
it was screeching

and I halted
in the middle of the room
hours after the fact

in another state.

# *Leather Jacket*

In the clearance rack
half-way down
on the wrong rack
not on sale at all
hanging where it
doesn't belong

is the leather jacket
I can't walk past
because Terri died
in a black leather jacket
like the one
I am crunching
in my fist

that like a heart
constricts and tightens.

I search the racks to fill the void.
There is nothing worth wanting;
no peace in any purchase.

## *Halloween*

Mother sent me to the Armory
with the rest of the children
in a gunnysack dress
a belt around my waist
moccasins on my feet and
pheasant feathers
in a band around my head.

We were formed into groups
performing rituals
circling for judgment
the best to be chosen
blue ribbon granted
and I took it home.

My sister took the feathers I wore for
a crown of her own the year after that.
Came home with second place.

There's a story that lives past win,
a word that means one, not the other.

Fast forward decades.

We dressed for success, worked long
hours, raised tall children, put them
in costumes, told tall tales.
Stories live on.

The costumes we wore, fell away.

# *Speech*
    *(in memory of Charles A. Elkin)*

After four months in a coma,
he starts trying

to move his mouth around in
painful efforts.

He seeks re-entry into this
earth world; he seeks it

because he is as afraid of
that other world as we are of

his survival chances in this one.
We are all on edge.

He lies there twitching; mumbles
out. Everyone is excited.

Unexpectedly, every so often,
his leg jerks up to his chest.

Every once in a while a word
comes out clear,

"Shit."

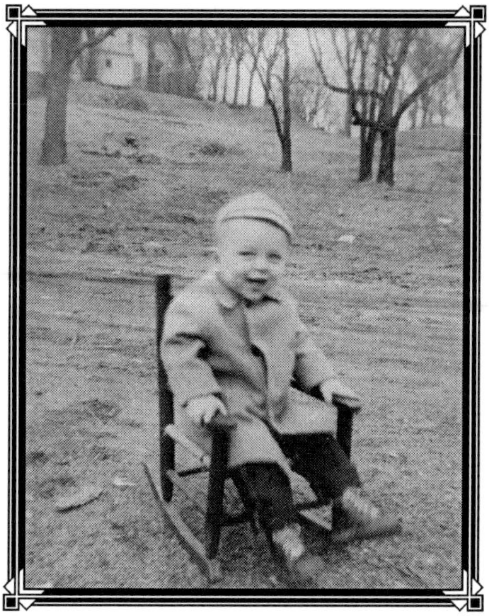

# *Thrill Seeker*

Back behind the house
take the path that leads
past the bench nailed
between two trees.
Veer to the left. Stay
on top of the hill.

Don't go down into the hollow
but stay on the ridge
that circles the valley.
On your left, circle around
to the tree opposite
where you entered the woods.

Your brother will be there.
He will have tied a large knot
in the rope that swings
from a branch of the tree
and you will sit on the knot.

He will make sure it is tight.
You will swing like the boys.
You will swing higher than before
and drop when you are ready.

Your stomach will catch in your throat.
You will learn to land on your own two feet.

## *Bookshelf*

A buzz of her saw
the blade cuts
along a pencilled line

four 8-foot boards and others
in 2-foot strips lay crosswise
on the oak slats of the hardwood floor

she thinks of spacing and
the distance she will need

she thinks of men and how this world
is waiting for their designs

she remembers the smirk on
her brother's face when he
got out of husking corn

she thinks of all the things
girls aren't supposed to do

knows something good
will come of this cutting

tiny chips fall
she feels the wind of the whirr
an opening behind the blade

it may take a while
for the dust to settle.

# In Search Of

# *A Taste For Chocolate*

I see the small girl following her older brother. She is tagging after him to the cement slab where he will pick up the bucksaw that cuts the long grasses on the north side of the house where the mower can't go. She is following him all this way for a taste of his chocolate ice cream cone. She is four or five.

I see the small girl sitting on the formica table. The mother is frantically running back and forth from the bathroom sink to the table where she wipes blood from the little girl's face and rinses the washcloth in the sink, returning over and over again until she is sure the cut is not near the eye. On the nose, a half moon. A circle not quite completed by the hollow tubular end of the bucksaw that swung back from the arm of the brother.

The little girl is quiet. I can't see that she's crying.

She's still hungry.

# *The Hunt for Asparagus*

Asparagus is best if you find it early Spring when it is young and fresh, not like it gets later—spread out and spindly. I knew the places it came up year after year—in the lot to the left of our property, then under two trees, then over to the cement where my brother played basketball. After that, beyond the bench nailed between two trees, a clump on the hill. As I went further into the woods, I would find another clump here and there. More of a guessing game now because it changed each year.

Once in the woods it was hard to tell where asparagus would grow and you could forget what you came for. The earth became our playground. A tree stump became a chair. Branches became boundaries, walls for an imaginary house—leaves were always the cushion. Inside the forest there were no rules, no adults. Inside this freedom we witnessed seasons pass and saw the changes a forest goes through. We grew in the space of the trees, the immense sky, the warm sun. We discovered our limits in our own backyard.

We spoke the language of the leaves and left traces of where we had been on the earth's floor. We wanted to find our way back to the same wilderness. We wanted the same freedom over and over. We wanted to keep this secret. We wanted always to return.

Every year I came back to the same places in this hunt for asparagus. When I'd bring the asparagus to Mom she was always pleased with the young stalks, children of the field.

We went into the moist undertones of life because there were discoveries to make and we were springing up like weeds—young enough to believe no one had done this before. We were on the edge of a dream and we stepped inside without fear. We treasured what we found. Even broken glass resembling a boat was exquisite in its design and we saved it in a cigar box. We would have gone deeper into the woods but this was all the further we needed to go. The land was marked. The territory we explored had boundaries. Every so often we emerged from the trees into the sunlight. We were surprised by the immenseness of the field just beyond the forest.

We were in our element at the creek where long grasses stuck to our legs on hot summer days. We sat on the edge of the bank and watched the water and the waterlilies rock on the water *yet stay in the place they were rooted* with long and tenuous roots in the earth below. They touched that earth and grew, took their food from the earth and sky. We took this in. It was our own nourishment. We tentatively walked the edges then turned to climb the oak tree where the view was better. Up in the corner of the branches, in the deep V of the tree we were safe and in the center of things. We spent hours in the vastness of this one small creekbed. We thought time was endless.

Edges are always the problem. To cross or not to cross. How deep is the water? How muddy the stream?

Walking those fields, childhood swiftly passing, everything was new, everything was becoming old. Right before our eyes trees were falling.

## *Downstream*

barefoot    crosseyed    bookworm

quackgrass    pathway    underfoot
featherweight    dragonfly    overhead

milkweed    lilypad    creekbed
loudmouth    heartfelt    frogsong

overcome    swampland    waterflow
understand    undercurrent    tomboy

# Breathing Lessons

## *Emergence*

is coming out of the warming house.
It is skating on ice,

a leap into crisp winter, the
shakiness of a thin blade to stand on.

All eyes will be on your steady
glide, the push
from the edge of the ice
to the center of attention.

Grace is a gift,
a talent for keeping your balance.
Sharpen your blade.
Begin with a scratch, cut
an impression, a figure eight.

Give them something to look at.
Spin if you must.

## *Vacation*

I dream of the clams we opened
on the shores of Eau Claire Lake:
how we tugged and pulled to
pry open hinge
poked and prodded
pulled back muscle
lips, layers
to open halves against their will
against all the strength of the mussel.

Nothing prepared us for the opening.
The loss of the dream.
The pearl that never was.

Walking away we dropped
empty shells, broken,
scattered among rock, water,
half in, half out—what did we care

the Jacques Cousteau dream
of riches from the sea
washed away.

I remember how we
got back home:
scaling the hill sideways—
how the rocks crumbled at our feet.

## *Breathing Lessons*

Acknowledge the reason you left the house
to walk the path of the creek.

Take notice of the long quackgrass
the humid way it grazes your leg.

Know that the meandering creek
yields secrets. Go to it. Find the
center of its turnings.

You are in the midst of your youth,
deep in the woods. You have
brought your lunch. It is simple
but nourishing. It is all you need.

You are gathering the strength you
will need to climb the tree.
You are out on a limb.
You are over the water.

You cannot see how far it flows
or when it becomes a river.

You do not know what ocean
it empties into,
only that you will rise up

out of the ocean like a whale
memories cascading off your
rising back. Each exhalation
a fountain of release.

## *Silence*

is underwater.
It is gliding through chlorine
swift and neat,

a sleek push
from the side of a pool.

There is silence in the knowing,
the holding of breath.
Silence in the ducking down,
the slip below the
clear edge of the surface.

You push your way up
rise from the depths
like a torpedo
and there is even silence
in this, the shoot
through the water
no one can hear.

Rely on your instincts.
Do not breathe until you have risen
above the edge of the water
that once held you down
and now lets you rise.

To rest, float. Let your arms
be weightless at your side.
Allow the part of you to surface
that wants to rise.

NANCY FREDERIKSEN grew up in New Richmond, Wisconsin and currently resides in Coon Rapids, Minnesota. Her poems have appeared in Great River Review, Calyx, Zone 3, The North Stone Review and other literary journals. In 1997, she was awarded a Jerome Foundation Travel and Study Grant to further a manuscript of poetry based on Andrew Wyeth's *Helga Pictures* and a residency at Harmony Women's Fund, Norcroft Retreat Center on Lake Superior. She enjoys writing, playing guitar, many artforms and spending time with family and friends.